A Servant of
CHRIST

#5

The Single Sermon Series

A Servant of CHRIST

James Alan Lynch

Publishing
Angel
Climbing

A Servant of Christ
Written by James Alan Lynch

Transcribed and edited by Lisa Soland
Text copyright © 2024 James Alan Lynch

Published in 2024 by:
Climbing Angel Publishing
PO Box 32381
Knoxville, Tennessee 37930
http://www.ClimbingAngel.com

First Edition: February 2024
Printed in the United States of America

Graphic Design: Climbing Angel Publishing

ISBN: 978-1-956218-30-5
Library of Congress Control Number: 2024900426

This book is dedicated to...

The Senior Adults at West Park Baptist Church,
from whom I have learned much about being
a servant of Christ.

*"You shall stand up before the gray head and
honor the face of an old man, and you shall fear
your God: I am the Lord."*
(Leviticus 19:32)

OUR SCRIPTURE

17 And he said to his disciples, "Temptations to sin are sure to come, but woe to the one through whom they come! 2 It would be better for him if a millstone were hung around his neck and he were cast into the sea than that he should cause one of these little ones to sin. 3 Pay attention to yourselves! If your brother sins, rebuke him, and if he repents, forgive him, 4 and if he sins against you seven times in the day, and turns to you seven times, saying, 'I repent,' you must forgive him." 5 The apostles said to the Lord, "Increase our faith!" 6 And the Lord said, "If you had faith like a grain of mustard seed, you could say to this mulberry tree, 'Be uprooted and planted in the sea,' and it would obey you. 7 "Will any one of you who has a servant plowing or keeping sheep say to him when he has come in from the field, 'Come at once and recline at table'? 8 Will he not rather say to him, 'Prepare supper for me, and dress properly, and serve me while I eat and drink, and afterward you will eat and drink'? 9 Does he thank the servant because he did what was commanded? 10 So you also, when you have done all that you were commanded, say, 'We are unworthy servants; we have only done what was our duty.'"

(Luke 17:1-10)

Are You
A Servant of Christ?

Some time ago, my oldest daughter, Megan, and her husband took their family out west to Scottsdale, Arizona, for medical treatment. There was a wonderful family there who allowed my daughter and her family to stay with them while Megan received her treatment. This couple was probably mine and my wife, Kathy's age—in their late 50s, maybe early 60s. They decided to adopt Megan's four kids as their grandchildren, too, and gave them Christmas gifts. It was a blessing to know that somebody loved our family like that during a difficult time.

Megan's two youngest children are twin boys—Isaac and Elijah. They were four and a half years old at the time. Recently, they were talking about this Arizona couple, and one of the twins commented on the woman, claiming she was going to have a baby. Megan, their mother, explained to the kids that this woman was Grandmommy and Poppy's age. She concluded the conversation by stating that this

1

older woman would not have a baby. The six-year-old replied, "But she has black hair." So, ladies, according to this six-year-old, if you are still dying your hair, you can still have babies.

Things are not always as they appear, and they are not always as they appear because we sometimes don't have all the information. Or maybe we don't fully understand the information we do have.

When asked to preach on the verses of Luke 17:1-10, I thought that it would be nice if I could break those verses up into three sermons. At first, they didn't seem to have anything to do with each other. However, in the process of putting my notes together, I came to discover that they do. These ten verses have everything to do with each other. The key to understanding the first six verses is the last four. Jesus is talking about being His servant. So, as we work through these verses, you will be asked three primary questions that will help us explore where we are along the path to obedience.

Do you have a proper view of sin?

For by grace you have been saved through faith. And this is not your own doing; it is the gift of God, not a result of works, so that no one may boast.
(Ephesians 2:8-9)

If we legitimately understand that we are saved by grace through faith without works, we sometimes have the tendency to gloss over the seriousness of sin. This misdirect is not something we can blame on a misunderstanding of the grace of God from the Word of God. It is our human nature to vacillate from believing one extreme to the other.

I become overwhelmed when I think about all Jesus has done for me. When He tore that veil in the temple, Jesus opened the way for me and you, gentiles and sinners, to have direct access to the Holy One, to God. If we were raised in a Christian home, never rebelled much, and have always been a "good girl or boy," we can sometimes miss the wickedness and depravity that exists in our hearts. Sin is serious. Sin is an offense against a holy, sinless God. Sin is so serious that Jesus deals with it solemnly in these first four verses of Luke 17. He wants us to realize the serious nature of sin, and we are also to be very careful not to cause others to sin.

> *Temptations to sin are sure to come, but woe to the one through whom they come! It would be better for him if a millstone were hung around his neck and he were cast into the sea than that he should cause one of these little ones to sin.*
> (Luke 17:1-2)

That's pretty serious talk!

If you've been a Christian for a while, you've read these verses repeatedly. But if we're not careful, the words lose their impact. A millstone was used to grind grain. It would have been extremely heavy. If that millstone had been placed around your neck and you were thrown into the sea, you would sink to the bottom. You would be unable to breathe and trying to gasp for air, and you would be terrified. If you've ever had a time when you couldn't catch your breath, you know that can be a frightening experience.

Imagine if you were connected to this stone, dragged under the water, and not strong enough to escape. You would know that you were about to drown. As you were trying desperately to hold your breath, you would be thinking, *"If I could just get up to the top of the water!"* But you're being dragged down to the bottom, and it's horrific. Jesus said that it would be better to have that happen to you than if you were to cause someone else to sin. We are to be extra careful not to cause others to sin.

How could we cause someone else to sin? Well, by *our sin*. We can set an example for others—good or bad. When reading Luke 17:2, we think of our children because Jesus says, "Little ones." But Jesus is not explicitly referring to *little children*. Jesus is talking about people who you might affect. The "little one" could apply to the person sitting beside you. It doesn't have to be a little child. It could be anyone, and we're all His *little ones*.

Jesus said it would be better if a millstone were tied around our neck and we were dragged down to the bottom of the sea than for us to cause someone else to sin. When you or I sin, it is always an act of selfishness. Our sinning is about us, and when we think about how our sin directly affects those around us, we should be impacted. We are accountable for causing others to sin, so we must take our own sin seriously. And when it occurs, our sin must be confronted. But we need to be sure to address *all* sin when it happens.

"Pay attention to yourselves! If your brother sins, rebuke him, and if he repents, forgive him."
(Luke 17:3)

Why is it important to rebuke our brother or sister is he or she sins? Because we're here for one another. We want to avoid causing someone else to sin and help one another to *not* do so. So when one of us sins, our brother needs to confront us. If we are blinded to the sin that we are committing, someone needs to confront us.

I don't know about you, but I don't want anybody in my business. But we must remember that it is necessary to allow your brother or sister in Christ to confront *your* sin. But it must be done lovingly, carefully, and humbly, lest the confronter also be tempted.

> *Brothers, if anyone is caught in any transgression, you who are spiritual should restore him in a spirit of gentleness. Keep watch on yourself, lest you too be tempted.*
> (Galatians 6:1)

Sin must be confronted because sin is serious. Then, we are to work to repair the relationship damage caused by the sin. If we rebuke our brother "and if he sins against you seven times in the day, and turns to you seven times, saying, 'I repent,' you must forgive him" (Luke 17:4).

The whole point of confronting sin is *reconciliation*. It's not *judging* someone. It's not putting someone else down. Sin separates; forgiveness reconciles.

Maybe someone has sinned against you, and you are bitter. Perhaps you haven't done anything about it. Well, you need to repent because what you are doing is a sin. The Bible says you must rebuke him. Do it in love and work toward reconciliation because sin is damaging. It divides.

If someone sins against you seven times a day, and you keep confronting them, and they keep repenting, well, that will get a little tiresome after a while, right? Well, how often in a day does Jesus forgive you? We are to have the same attitude toward forgiveness of sin toward others as Jesus has toward us. This is a *proper view of sin*.

- SECOND QUESTION -
Do you practice a biblical faith?

Right after Jesus set the bar of forgiveness in Luke 17:4, the apostles made a request.

> *The apostles said to the Lord, "Increase our faith!" And the Lord said, "If you had faith like a grain of mustard seed, you could say to this mulberry tree, 'Be uprooted and planted in the sea,' and it would obey you."*
> (Luke 17:5-6)

Why are the apostles saying, "Lord, increase our faith!"? Because they understand that if they have to deal with sin by forgiving, it will take faith. If we have to put this forgiveness into practice, it will require an act of faith. We will need faith because Jesus is not talking about forgiving only seven times. And if you keep a notebook where you are marking down those sins against you, and suddenly it is the eighth time this same person has sinned against you, you can't say, *"Eight! That's it. I don't have to forgive the eighth time because Jesus said only seven."* That is not the spirit of what Jesus is saying. If you are keeping records, you know what you're *not* doing? You're not forgiving.

> *Then came Peter to him, and said, Lord, how oft shall my brother sin against me, and I forgive him? till seven times? Jesus saith unto him, I say not unto thee, Until seven times: but, Until seventy times seven.*
> (Matthew 18:21-22 KJV)

So, the idea is not to simply forgive seven or even seventy times seven. *"Wow. 490! I'm finished!"* If Jesus only forgave us 490 times, we would have been in hell a long time ago. The forgiveness Jesus speaks of is to be complete and continual. Sin has to be dealt with, and one needs faith to do it. That's why the disciples asked Jesus to increase their faith. It takes faith in an all-powerful God to be able to forgive.

Jesus' answer seems a little odd. He doesn't say, *"Okay, I grant you greater faith."* What does He say?

> *And the Lord said, "If you had faith like a grain of mustard seed, you could say to this mulberry tree, 'Be uprooted and planted in the sea,' and it would obey you."*
> (Luke 17:6)

I have heard a lot of sermons on the mustard seed, as I'm certain you have. One can get pretty elaborate on the subject. You can talk about all the seed's characteristics, etc. I'm not going to spend a lot of time on the mustard seed, but I do want to point out that Jesus refers to this tiny seed five times in the New Testament, and each time He compares it to something. Here, the mustard seed is compared to *faith*, but Jesus also compares the mustard seed to the *Kingdom of God*.

In Luke 13, Jesus compares a mustard seed to the Kingdom of Heaven. Pay particular attention to the mustard seed's qualities or properties.

> *He said therefore, "What is the kingdom of God like? And to what shall I compare it? It is like a grain of mustard seed that a man took and sowed in his garden, and it grew and*

became a tree, and the birds of the air made nests in its branches." And again he said, "To what shall I compare the kingdom of God?"
(Luke 13:18-20)

Jesus is comparing the Kingdom of Heaven, the Kingdom of God, to a mustard seed, and He gives you two basic properties of the mustard seed that He is using for this comparison.

First, the mustard seed is *small*, and a man took and sowed it in his garden. But it also has great *potential*. The mustard seed can grow, and this tree comes up, and birds can rest in the branches of the tree produced by this tiny little seed.

Jesus is saying that a mustard seed is not only like the Kingdom of God but also like faith. Faith can be small. Notice how the apostles said, "Increase our faith," and Jesus didn't just wave His hand and say, *"Your faith is now increased."* But He did say, *"If you had a tiny amount of faith, you could move trees just by that faith."* In other words, *"You could take a tiny amount of faith and accomplish great things."*

How is that possible? Remember what the man back in Chapter 13 did with that mustard seed? He *sowed* the mustard seed. In other words, he used, exercised, and planted the mustard seed. Do you see what Jesus is saying? We have to *plant* our faith. We have to *exercise* our faith. Don't wait to act in faith until you have more faith. Use the faith you have. Act on the faith you have right now!

Do you remember what Jesus' half-brother James said? "Faith without works is dead."

"What good is it, my brothers, if someone says he has faith but does not have works? Can that faith save him? 15 If a brother or sister is poorly clothed and lacking in daily food, 16 and one of you says to them, "Go in peace, be warmed and filled," without giving them the things needed for the body, what good is that? 17 So also faith by itself, if it does not have works, is dead. 18 But someone will say, "You have faith and I have works." Show me your faith apart from your works, and I will show you my faith by my works. 19 You believe that God is one; you do well. Even the demons believe—and shudder! 20 Do you want to be shown, you foolish person, that faith apart from works is useless? 21 Was not Abraham our father justified by works when he offered up his son Isaac on the altar? 22 You see that faith was active along with his works, and faith was completed by his works; 23 and the Scripture was fulfilled that says, "Abraham believed God, and it was counted to him as righteousness"—and he was called a friend of God. 24 You see that a person is justified by works and not by faith alone. 25 And in the

*same way was not also Rahab the prostitute
justified by works when she received the
messengers and sent them out by another
way? 26 For as the body apart from the spirit is
dead, so also faith apart from works is dead."*
(James 2:14-26)

We are saved by faith without works, but the
faith that saves us, works. If your faith does
not work, your faith is dead. You may assent to
a creed, but you do not have faith if you do not
act on the faith that you have.

So, when the disciples are concerned
about dealing with sin and they ask Jesus to
give them more faith because they can't do it,
Jesus says to act on the faith they do have, and
with that faith (regardless of how tiny) they
will do great things!

- THIRD QUESTION -
Do you live in humble dependence?

Jesus talks about the mustard seed faith—you
can do great things with this mustard seed
faith. He then goes right into this parable:

> *"Will any one of you who has a servant
> plowing or keeping sheep say to him when
> he has come in from the field, 'Come at
> once and recline at table'? Will he not*

*rather say to him, 'Prepare supper for me,
and dress properly, and serve me while I
eat and drink, and afterward you will eat
and drink'? Does he thank the servant
because he did what was commanded?"*
(Luke 17:7-9)

This parable is about someone who has a
servant but not a *specific type* of servant.
Notice that Jesus says, *"You who has a
servant plowing or keeping sheep."* He is
talking about someone who has a servant who
comes in from performing whatever duties
they have been given in the field. Then Jesus
asks a question about the master of that
servant, and the implication is that the answer
is "no."

We would not invite this servant to sit
beside us and recline at the table immediately.
Why? Because he's a servant. He has a job to
do. When he comes in from the field, whether
plowing or caring for the sheep, he is still a
servant. He has responsibilities, and part of
those responsibilities is caring for the master.
He's to feed the master first. So, Jesus says,

*"Will he not rather say to him, 'Prepare
supper for me, and dress properly, and serve
me while I eat and drink, and afterward you
will eat and drink'?"*
(Luke 17:8)

13

In other words, *"Once you have done all those things, you can sit down and eat. You are a servant, and the job of a servant is to take care of the bidding of the master."*

This story has two characters—the servant and the master. The servant is any type of servant. He could be one who takes care of the sheep or plows. He could be preaching a sermon or acting as an usher. He could be someone who cleans the church building or someone whose ministry is to pray because they are unable to leave the house. The servant could be any type of servant of the King. So, the servant's job is to do whatever the servant does, and the servant does all he is commanded.

Then we have the master, and the master is to be compared with Jesus. Jesus is our master, and we are His servants. He's the Lord and King. And so what does the master do? Well, he has absolute authority over the servant. The master can tell the servant anything that the servant is required to do, and because the servant belongs to the master, he is bound by duty to obey the master. Because he belongs to the master, he is a servant; not just an employee.

I don't know about you, but my mama taught me to say, "Thank you." Jesus asks, "Does he thank the servant?"

When I go to a restaurant and the server brings me my food, I always respond by saying, "Thank you." But that's a little different relationship, though. That's not a servant/master relationship. This is culturally difficult for us to identify with, but the relationship described here is a servant/master relationship. The master owns the servant. In our case, Jesus is the master and owns us in two ways.

First of all, He owns us because He made us. We wouldn't even exist had He not created us.

There's a story about a little boy who made a boat. He carved this boat out of wood and worked diligently to make it. When finished, he added a sail and put it into a stream. As the wind caught the sail, the boat began to pick up speed. The little boy kept trying to recapture the boat, but it finally went too far downstream, and he lost it. The boy was very sad because he had worked so hard to make his little boat. He loved that boat; he made that boat. But that boat was now lost.

Sometime later, the little boy was in town and noticed his beloved boat in a local store window for sale. It had a price tag on it. The little boy told the shop owner that the boat in the store window was his. The shop owner said, "Well, son, it's for sale, and here's the price." So, the little boy began working hard to earn the money to bring the boat home to its rightful owner. When he was finally able to purchase his boat back, he held it in his hand and said, "Now, you're twice mine. First, I made you, and now I have bought you." In much the same way, Jesus made us. We were created in His image and for His purpose, but we, too, have sailed away from our Creator.

> *In the beginning was the Word, and the Word was with God, and the Word was God. He was in the beginning with God.* ***All things were made through him, and without him was not any thing made that was made.***
> (John 1:1-3)

Jesus made it all. He is the creator, but we have strayed from Him. We have sailed away from Him because of our sin.

> ***All we like sheep have gone astray; we have turned—every one—to his own way;*** *and the Lord has laid on him the iniquity of us all.*
> (Isaiah 53:6)

Jesus came to this earth. The King of kings and the Lord of lords lived as a servant. He became obedient even unto death on the cross, to take our place and purchase us back at the price of His own blood. Now, if you're a

Christian, you're twice His. You belong to Him. He is your master.

Some years ago, I remember a debate about "lordship salvation." You don't hear much about that anymore. Is Jesus your Savior, or is Jesus your Lord? Well, let me tell you—He is both.

Jesus does not have a split personality. When you receive Jesus as your Savior, He is the Lord. You can't choose what aspect of His character you take into your life. "*I want Him to save me. I want Him to forgive my sin, but I don't want Him telling me what to do.*" You don't get to do that. Yes, we are saved by grace, through faith, without works.

> *For by grace you have been saved through faith. And this is not your own doing; it is the gift of God, not a result of works, so that no one may boast.*
> (Ephesians 2:8-9)

It is absolutely true that we are saved by grace alone, through faith alone, in Christ alone! It is also true that when this Jesus moves into your life, He is King. He is Lord. If you think you are simply getting a ticket to Heaven, and can say to Him, "*Thanks for saving me, Lord, but don't bother me again until I get to Heaven,*" you will have a rude awakening one day. We are His servants, and

He is our master. We belong to Him. This is what Jesus is talking about.

> *"So you also, when you have done all that you were commanded, say, 'We are unworthy servants; we have only done what was our duty.'"*
> (Luke 17:10)

I prayed quite a bit while studying this passage, and I read the verses over and over again. "We are unworthy servants." The King James uses the word "unprofitable." "We are unprofitable servants..."

I have a business and understand profit. (Actually, I understand the *lack of profit* more than I understand *profit*.) "Profit" is when you invest in something—your work, a product, or a stock. You invest a certain amount of dollars, and anything over what you invest is profit. That is how "business" and "profit" are supposed to work.

But we do not bring any profit to God. Perhaps this is a bit shocking to you. Maybe you are saying to yourself, *"That's not a very nice thing to say."* You are precious to your Heavenly Father, but this does not erase the fact that you and I do not bring Him any gain. In other words, we do not add anything back to God for His investment in us.

God did not save us to get something out of it. Jesus shed His blood for you in order to purchase you back from the slave market of sin. That is how precious you are to Him. However, we have nothing to add to Him as a return on His investment.

If you are a Christian, you are only a Christian because Jesus gave everything He had for you. He loves you that much. Jesus didn't love you for what He would get out of the relationship. He loves you simply because that is who He is. *Jesus is love.*

I prayed about this too, and thought, *"Lord, I can't even say that I have done all that was commanded of me. I mean, if I had done all that was commanded of me, You're telling me, even then, I am an unworthy servant. But I haven't even done that. I'm less than unworthy."* But Jesus loved me anyway. He loves *all of us* anyway. And He has shown us such grace!

If we are not servants of God to provide Him some sort of gain, then why are we called "His servants?" We serve Him out of gratitude because of what He has done for us. But we are no less His servants, and as servants of God, we must have a proper view of sin. We must exercise the faith He has given us, and we must humbly depend on Him because we are nothing without Him. Jesus said, "Apart from Me, you can do nothing."

*"I am the vine; you are the branches.
Whoever abides in me and I in him, he it is
that bears much fruit, for apart from me
you can do nothing."*
(John 15:5)

As servants of Christ, we must recognize that if we grow in our ability to identify and adequately deal with sin, if we grow in our ability to exercise our faith, it's not us. It's Him. It's Him in us. Paul said,

*For I know that nothing good dwells in me, that
is, in my flesh. For I have the desire to do what
is right, but not the ability to carry it out.*
(Romans 7:18)

As we recognize our sinfulness before God, we cannot help but give Him glory for the great grace that He has given to us. Let's face it; we're a ragtag bunch of misfits, but regardless, Jesus loves us. And if there is any good thing in me, if there is any good thing in you, it's not us. It's Jesus working through us. We must completely depend on Him. He is our King, our Lord, our Master. He owns us. He purchased us with His own blood.

If you are reading these words today, and you have not received Jesus as your Savior and your Lord, I'm inviting you right now to do so. But more importantly, Jesus is inviting you!

Perhaps you are thinking, *"This Jesus sounds like a taskmaster!"* But nothing could be further from the truth. He is a loving King, a loving Savior, who gave everything so you could know Him, have your sins forgiven, and obtain authentic purpose in your life!

Always remember, He created you and knows you better than you even know yourself. You can absolutely trust Him to lead you through this life and into the next.